T0132222

Understanding Culture Awareness

LUCY NKWAMENI NJOMO BEM

AuthorHouse™
1663 Liberty Drive
Bloomington, IN 47403
www.authorhouse.com
Phone: 1 (800) 839-8640

Published by AuthorHouse 05/28/2019

ISBN: 978-1-5462-9575-4 (sc)
ISBN: 978-1-5462-9576-1 (e)

Print information available on the last page.

Any people depicted in stock imagery provided by Getty Images are models,
and such images are being used for illustrative purposes only.
Certain stock imagery © Getty Images.

This book is printed on acid-free paper.

Because of the dynamic nature of the Internet, any web addresses or links contained in this book may have changed
since publication and may no longer be valid. The views expressed in this work are solely those of the author and do
not necessarily reflect the views of the publisher, and the publisher hereby disclaims any responsibility for them.

authorHOUSE®

Understanding Cultural Awareness

LUCY NKWAMENI NJOMO, BEM

CULTURE

The term Culture is used by social scientists for a people's whole way of life. Culture consists of all the ideas, objects and ways of doing things created by the group. Cultural includes arts, beliefs, customs, inventions, language, technology and traditions. A culture is any way of life, simple or complex.

Culture consists of learned ways of acting, feeling and thinking rather than biologically determined ways, some simple animals act on the basis of information carried in their genes, the parts of a cell that determine inherited traits. This biologically inherited information even includes the animal's ways of obtaining food and work out their ways of doing these things, a process that never ends. Culture is a set of simple extensions of various part of the body.

Without culture the astronauts could not have reached the moon nor survived there. The human body needs oxygen and a certain range of temperature to live. However culture devices have enabled human beings to overcome some of the limitations of their bodies and stay alive in harsh environments. Early culture was a means to extend the ability to obtain food, seek protection and raise offspring.

The ancestors of modern human being had an advantage in the struggle for survival because they developed tools and other culture. They became more likely to live and reproduce than creatures that lacked such advantages. As a result the ability to create culture grew from generation to generation.

Every family has a culture and tradition of its own. This tradition includes many traits that the family shares with others who live in the same area with belong to the same social class. In addition, the family has its own set of cultural traits.

All cultures have features that result from basic needs shared by all people. Every culture has methods of obtaining food and shelter. It has an orderly means of distributing the food and other goods to its people. Each culture has systems for assigning power and responsibility, including social ranks and governments. There is also a way to keep order and settle disputes for instance, a system of police, courts and prisons. Every culture has ways to protect itself against invaders. It also has family relationships including forms of marriage and systems of kinship. A culture has religious beliefs and a set of practices to express them. All societies have forms of artistic expression such as carving, painting and music. In addition each culture has some type of scientific knowledge. This knowledge may be folklore about the plants people eat and the animals they hunt or it may be a highly developed science.

WHAT IS CULTURE?

The culture of a society is the totality of its shared beliefs, norms, values, rituals, language, history, knowledge and social character. It implies those things that are conscious, that are kept in being only because we choose to maintain them. Although many elements of our culture are apparently outside our control (e.g. we are born into a language which we more or less automatically adopt) there is a sense in which we can change our culture. Culture is a human creation into which we are socialised and which we can, with some effort, change (The SAGE Dictionary of Sociology, 2006)

Therefore, culture is

- dynamic and evolving
- learned and passed on through generations
- shared among those who agree on the way they name and understand reality

The iceberg model can be used to help us to understand what culture is. The top of the iceberg, that part above the water represents that part of culture that is seen to all e.g. the food we eat, the way we dress, the music we listen to and the way we treat illnesses. However, there are other parts of culture that's less visible e.g. our values and beliefs about how and why people suffer ill health.

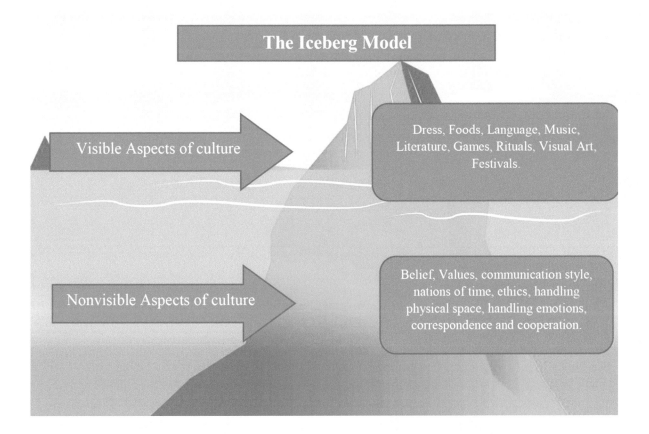

The Iceberg Model

Visible Aspects of culture

Dress, Foods, Language, Music, Literature, Games, Rituals, Visual Art, Festivals.

Nonvisible Aspects of culture

Belief, Values, communication style, nations of time, ethics, handling physical space, handling emotions, correspondence and cooperation.

Cultures is like icebergs, are defined more by what is unseen than seen. This model was developed by anthropologist Edward T. Hall in the 1970s

The iceberg model of understanding culture, you can observe about 10% of culture, but to comprehend the rest, you have to go deeper.

The visible aspects of culture are important parts of how cultures interact and maintain their sense of unity.

When you first interact with a new culture, maybe through travel or other experiences, this is the part of culture that is immediately evident to you.

The top 10% of the culture iceberg have a relatively low emotional load, that can be changed and altered without fundamentally challenging the existence of a culture or people's ideas about who they are.

The invisible aspects of culture are like nonverbal communication, how we interact with or show our emotions, our concepts of personal space, our definitions of beauty, and our basic ideas about manners and contextual behaviour.

This part of society takes more time for an outsider to understand because it's not as obviously visible. It also carries a heavier emotional load. Once you begin to change these values, people begin to feel like their cultural identity is being threatened.

Our culture and health practices are inextricably linked and bounded together. People all over the world approach their health in many different ways and it is heavily influenced by their culture. For instance, a parent may believe that their child's illness is caused by an evil spirit, 'evil eye' or demon. This may then result in the parent seeking help from a faith leader as oppose to a medical doctor.

In some communities some people may choose to treat an illness in ways that it has always been treated for centuries, which might be considered harmful by professionals.

CULTURAL AWARENESS

Culture is the customary beliefs, social forms, and material traits of a racial, religious, or social group also the characteristic features of everyday existence as diversions or a way of life shared by people in a place

Culture influences many parts of people's lives including: Food, dress, opinions, identity, music, buildings, manners, social interaction, and language. We need to understand each other's cultural backgrounds to make sense of different viewpoints and opinions.

Cultural Awareness is important in creating cross cultural understanding and acceptance. Cultural awareness gives us a better understanding of our culture.

Culture makes up a large part of our day to day life. Cultural differences include differences in food, clothes, religion and language. American Iced Tea for insatnce, thinks about the different ways different cultures take tea. English Tea, Chinese Tea Small differences, like the way each culture drinks tea can be difficult to get used to at first because these things are so important to our daily live.

However, the small things are just the tip of the iceberg-they are only the things we can see on the surface. There are many parts of culture that aren't visible. These include:

- Work Ethic
- Importance of Time
- Religious Beliefs
- Values
- Nature of Friendships.

Because these differences aren't visible they are very difficult to communicate and understand. Despite this, the parts of culture we cannot see are very important because they underpin the parts of culture we can see.

How to be culturally aware: Engage with other peoples' cultures by asking questions; Be Open! Don't get into the habit of thinking your way is the only way of doing things – rather think how is it done in another country; Think about what you can learn from other peoples, and what you can teach them. It is therefore important to invite others to share their culture with you.

Attitudes and Expectations Peoples will have a lot of questions before and after they arrive. Start to think about some of the answers to these questions and how you could answer them and will the language be good enough what will people look like? What will the weather look like? How do I open like? What will my accommodation be like? What will I do if I get ill? Will people be friendly? Etc.

Language Barrier sits is most likely that English will be a second language for the majority of international peoples. Some will have excellent English, while others will still be learning. Therefore, it is important to be aware of how to communicate effectively. How might this misunderstanding lead to future miscommunication?

Simplifying your language is not easy. It takes time and practice. One may even feel a little silly. However, simplifying your language when appropriate will help which will in turn increase confidence speaking.

To simplify a language, refrain from using long words, speak slowly and as clearly as possible, stress important words, don't be afraid to repeat yourself If one keeps making the same mistake correct her/him. They want to improve the language and they won't mind being corrected again and again.

Other ways of communicating are by non-verbal communication is just as important as verbal communication. Think about body language, posture, eye contact, facial expressions, gestures and tone of voice when talking. If one is really struggling to communicate with peoples, try some of the following: •Write it down• Use of hands to reinforce what you are saying, Use facial expressions to reinforce what is being said, • Try using different words or rephrase sentences

Culture shock is a condition of disorientation affecting someone who is suddenly exposed to an unfamiliar culture or way of life or set of attitudes. Migrations into foreign countries are particularly vulnerable because people are more isolated and lack their immediate support system. Some stages of are:

The Honeymoon Stage - The individual is very positive about the culture, is overwhelmed with impressions, finds the culture exotic and is fascinated by it.

The Independence Stage -: is largely passive and doesn't confront as the individual enjoys being in the culture

The Disintegration stage - the culture functions easily in the disintegration stage, now the individual begins to interact with cultural behaviour his/her finds to adopts the behaviour of the people.

The Autonomy Stage - individual begins to feel lonely without the support of friends understand more of the mentally and family behaviours of the people.

The Re-Integration Stage - in/encountering the culture as the individual begins to reject his/her culture and feel less isolated and regains the differences they are encountering: Sense of humour and feelings they are into but are getting more used to the change.

Cultural is all about:

Awareness

Acceptance

Respect

Cultural awareness is the understanding of the differences between themselves and people from other countries or other backgrounds, especially differences in attitudes and values.

Cultural acceptance is treating impartially and fairly each ethnic group without promoting the particular beliefs or values of any group. Indeed, cultural acceptance brings unity.

Cultural respect is to embrace and appreciate the differences and celebrate and leverage the similarities. Respect is the foundation of all positive successes that arise from living and working in a diverse environment.

CULTURES DIFFER

Culture differ in details from one part of the world to other, for insatnce eating is a biological need, but what people eat, when and how they eat and how food is prepared differ from culture to culture.

Environmental differences care related to cultural variations, such factors as climate, land farms, mineral resources and native and animals all influence culture. For instance, most people in tropical regions wear draped clothing which consists of one or more long pieces of cloth wrapped around the body. People who live in colder parts of the world wear tailored clothing which is cut and sewn to fit the body. Tailored clothing provides more warmth then draped clothing.

People do not realise how greatly culture influences their behaviour until they come across other ways of doing things. Only then can they see that they have been doing things in a cultural way rather than in a national way. For instance, many westerners believe it is natural to look directly into a person's eye while talking. But the people of some Asia/African nations think it is rude to do so.

People feel most comfortable within their own culture and they prefer the company of others who share their culture. When people have to deal with persons of another culture even small differences in behaviour may make them uneasy. The difficulty or uneasiness that people undergo when they leave their own culture and enter another is called shock.

CULTURE, HEALTH AND STIGMA

Different cultural health practices is understood generically as customary ways and beliefs handed down (usually by oral communication, ritual, and/or imitation) from the past for present action, tradition is an integral component of every family, group, organisation, and nation.

Our culture and health practices are inextricably linked and bounded together. People all over the world approach their health in many different ways and it is heavily influenced by their culture. For instance, a parent may believe that their child's illness is caused by an evil spirit, 'evil eye' or demon. This may then result in the parent seeking help from a faith leader as oppose to a medical doctor.

In some communities some people may choose to treat an illness in ways that it has always been treated for centuries, which might be considered harmful by professionals. Some of these health practices can include:

❖ Cao go (coin rubbing): this is an ancient Chinese practice where ointment in placed on a flat surface like a coin and then it is rubbed onto the skin, in a manner that causes bruising.

❖ Male circumcision: the removal of the foreskin that covers the penis. It can cause serious harm and result in last damage to the organ. It is done for cultural and religious reasons. There is some evidence that it can reduce the chances of the transmission of HIV but this is debated, as the research conducted is too small scale to make broad generalisations.

❖ Moxibustion: a traditional Chinese treatment that uses dried Artemisia argyi that's heated and applied to the acupuncture points. It has been used extensively in the Far East (Southeast Asia, Mongolia, China, India and Japan) for many centuries and for many kinds of diseases, including pleurisy, pneumonia, abdominal pain, chest pain and local pains, and is equivalent to the Western medicine practice of prescribing hot compresses as an anti-irritant to attract white blood cells and antibodies to the irritated area.

❖ Cupping: Glass cups are used; a drop of alcohol is placed in the cup, lit with a match and immediately applied to the area. These leave large marks usually 2–3 cm in diameter. Instantly, the flame goes out as the 20% oxygen is used up; the skin is sucked up into the cup and allowed to stay in place for a few minutes (creating a red area) and then pulled off. This process is sometimes associated with acupuncture.

❖ Hijama/Bloodletting: Hijama is also known as cupping or bloodletting therapy. It is a process of removing blood from the body and it is distinctive from the well-known practice of bloodletting or cupping because Hijama is governed by specific times that it should take place as well as specific points on the body that enhances health, detoxifies the body and builds up immunity.

❖ Hijama is actually an ancient treatment that originated in China thousands of years ago. This therapy was originally known as 'cupping' because of the use of the cup as a therapeutic tool. The practitioner pumps air into the cup, either manually or by means of a suction device, to create a vacuum.

❖ Anal/Genital Insertions (ginger): ginger and sometimes herbs are inserted in the anus. This can be done as a source of punishment as ginger will have a burning effect. However, it can also be used as a remedy for stomach complaints.

❖ Herbal Suppositories (to remove meconium): sometimes parents in certain communities may use herbs will cause new-born babies to poo. For them this is important as failure to poo for new-borns may indicate a health problem. Some of these herbal suppositories used may cause dehydration in babies.

❖ Uvula cutting: is the fleshy piece of tissue hanging down over your tongue toward the back of your mouth. It helps you to push food to the back of your throat. Uvulectomy, a procedure which consists of cutting part or the entire uvula, is a common practice in sub-Saharan Africa. It is practiced by traditional healers as a cure of throat problems. It is usually done before the age of 5 years old and can result in the following health consequences: hemorrhage, anemia, septicemia, tetanus, risk of the Human Immunodeficiency Virus (HIV) infection, and death.

❖ Eyelid insertion: This is a common practice in northern Ethiopia and parts of Nigeria. It is used as a treatment for eye disease (commonly eye infections). It is performed with a razor blade and often results in secondary skin infections and excessive bleeding.

❖ Nutritional violence/Force feeding: children could be held down by their carer/parent and forced feed. Solids could be liquidised, the child's mouth is forced open and the food is then poured down their throat. Children could also be beat or tortured until they have eaten what they have been fed. In some countries images of a health child is one that is obese and this could be interpreted as symbolising the wealth of the family. Additionally, ideas about what is considered to be an attractive woman in some context is associated with women of a larger size and this could be a reason for force feeding. Another reason for forced feeding could be associated concerns about parental past experiences of poverty where there was a lack of food available.

Different cultures add meaning to what is good or bad, right or wrong and this may even extend to how people perceive others as accepted or strange in relation to their health. Stigma usually refers to mark of disgrace associated to something e.g. health. In most societies there is a stigma attached to people with mental health problems. People with mental health problems are usually stigmatised and excluded by others. Therefore, it is important to think how someone might be stigmatised due to how their culture perceives their illness. This will play a part in influencing if they seek help or not as they could be afraid that others may find out about their illness.

WHY HARMFUL PRACTICES AND NOT HARMFUL TRADITIONAL PRACTICES

There are also some practices that specifically happen to women and girls that could result in health consequences. This is usually called harmful traditional practices. We shall now discuss look at the debate in the use of this term.

Although the term 'harmful traditional practices' is used in the literature and in the national Violence against Women and Girls Strategy (Home Office, 2016), there are a number of challenges presented by its usage. The word 'traditional' has been conflated with culture, which channels our understanding of it as being only experienced by Black and Minority Ethnic communities. For some reason, culture has become synonymous with this group, when it is in fact universal.

The word 'tradition' also implies that violence against women and girls is an accepted practice and consequently makes challenging such practices, within a violence against women and girl's context, difficult. By jettisoning the term 'traditional', these practices are no longer cloaked under the guise of custom and can then be seen as harmful and a human rights violation.

WHAT ARE HARMFUL PRACTICES?

As early as the 1950s, United Nations specialized agencies and human rights bodies began considering the question of harmful traditional practices affecting the health of women, in particular female genital mutilation. But these issues have not received consistent broader consideration, and action to bring about any substantial change has been slow or superficial. As early as in the 1950's UN agencies and human rights bodies began exploring the question of harmful practices affecting women and girls, in particular FGM.

The United Nations defines harmful traditional practices as:

"Forms of violence that have been committed against women in certain communities and societies for so long that these abuses are considered a part of accepted cultural practice. These violations include female genital mutilation or cutting (FGM), dowry murder, so-called honour killings, and early marriage. They lead to death, disabilities, and physical and psychological dysfunction for millions of women annually".

HARMFUL TRADITIONAL PRACTICES THAT AFFECT THE HEALTH OF WOMEN AND GIRLS.

- **Early marriage, Child marriage, child engagements** (Nikah): According to the UN, it is defined as a formal marriage or informal union before age 18. In many parts of the world parents encourage the marriage of their daughters while they are still children in hopes that the marriage will benefit them both financially and socially. In the UK a young person can get married at the age of 16 or 17 with their parents' consent. Early marriage is sanctioning rape within marriage as girls (boys can also be victims but to a lesser extent than girls) are unable to give consent to intercourse. They experience serious health consequences as they get pregnant at a young age and they are at increased risk of suffering domestic abuse.

- **Female Genital Mutilation:** comprises all procedures that involve partial or total removal of the external female genitalia, or other injury to the female genital organs for non-medical reasons
- **Dowry and Dowry violence:** A dowry is a payment (cash or a gift) by one family to another when a couple is about to be married. In some countries it is given by the groom's family to the bridegroom's family and vice-versa. For instance, although dowry has been banned in India since the Dowry Prohibition Act (1961) it is still common for families to pay a dowry, where the woman/girl's family pays the man/boy's family a dowry. In some cases, the cost of the dowry would increase with the age and education level of the girl. In some situations, there is strong bargaining between the families to decide on the dowry to be paid and if for instance the groom decides that the dowry was not fully paid he may be violent towards his partner and this may lead to the death of the woman.
- **Temporary marriage**, (short-term marriage): temporary marriages or short-term marriages is a practice performed within Shi'a Islam. This is a practice where a woman will be married to a man for a short period of days, weeks or months. A dowry is usually negotiated and paid to the woman or her family but more than like the latter will receive the payment. Originally, women considered as less desirable e.g. widows, divorced or sex workers were the ones most likely to find themselves in such arrangements. However, the practice is becoming more common in the UK and was the subject of a BBC report in 2013. The marriage is seen as a contract before a final decision is made on the suitability of the arrangement for the couple involved.
- **Widowhood rites:** a woman is blamed for the death of her husband and must prove her innocence by engaging in a number of distressing rituals such as drinking the water of

HARMFUL PRACTICES IN THE WEST

It can be argued that the situation of women in the rich industrialised nations of the West is vastly better than that of women in other parts of the world where they face blatant discrimination and subordination to men. In spite of this, it is important to recognise that women in the West still face subordination on many levels. There is the view that this subordination is more difficult to recognise due to modernity, especially the ways in which women themselves perpetuate practices which maintain their subordination to men.

HP is not only an issue for the Black and Asian Diaspora communities. None BME communities in the UK have always performed and still perform HPs. Having the view that it only happens in BME communities runs the risk of ghettoising the issue and could even result in caricaturing the culture of others. So there are many practices in the West that are no less cultural than practices performed elsewhere.

Creating such dichotomised beliefs run the risk of professionals imposing ethnocentric views that rank one's own cultural beliefs as superior to all others. A more sophisticate debate will acknowledge and recognise that the UK has had a long history of performing harmful practices and which continue to be practised in varying forms. Patriarchy also plays an important role in perpetuating these HPs.

Some Harmful Practices in the West:

- Corsetry: presents an unrealistic and sexualised image of women. It restricts movement, causes breathing difficulties and other health consequences.
- FGM: The Victorians performed clitoridectomy to cure epilepsy, nymphomania and hysteria.
- Forced marriages – arranges marriages in the royal family (Prince Charles and Lady Diana)
- Forcibly removing new born babies from mother perceived as being incapable of caring for them

Some harmful practices are not viewed as being as such because they are framed under the guise of being consumer 'choice', 'medicine' or 'fashion' and so create an illusion of acceptability.

If practices such as force feeding and FGM are seen as harmful when performed by one group, why should other practices at the other end of the continuum, which are equally harmful and performed in the UK by white communities, evade being labelled as cultural? An example of this is a Western woman's quest for slenderness by extreme dieting or starvation, as it can result in eating disorders and death. Pornography, although, not seen as cultural, has created a demand for non-therapeutic cosmetic surgery in the West for instance labiaplasty and genital piercing but the label of it being a harmful practice is not attached.

According to Jeffrey's (2005), even Western beauty practices, such as makeup and high-heeled shoes are decorated and altered 'to show that women are members of a subordinate class that exists for men's delight'.

DIFFERENT BELIEFS AND CULTURAL HEALTH PRACTICES.

Exploring how one's personal beliefs, values and attitudes all have an impact on the work we do with others. It will focus to understand own personal beliefs, values and attitudes through a set of meaningful discussions and activities. Time will also be spent understanding and developing insight into how to work effectively with others who may have different beliefs and values.

The culture of a society is the totality of its shared beliefs, norms, values, rituals, language, history, knowledge and social character. It implies those things that are conscious, that are kept in being only because we choose to maintain them. Although many elements of our culture are apparently outside our control (e.g. we are born into a language which we more or less automatically adopt) there is a sense in which we can change our culture. Culture is a human creation into which we are socialised and which we can, with some effort; change (The SAGE Dictionary of Sociology, 2006)

Therefore, culture is

- dynamic and evolving (subject to change)
- patterns of behaviour shared by a group that makes them different to others
- learned and passed on through generations
- shared among those who agree on the way they name and understand reality
- shapes people's behaviour

Acculturation: refers to a process by which a person incorporates aspects of a different culture into their own culture. This occurs through a group/person coming into contact with a foreign culture or through the influence of an 'outside" culture.

Superstitious Beliefs: "superstition" refers to the collective beliefs of a group of people that are considered by people outside this group to have no basis in reality or cannot be logically explained by scientific knowledge.

Values: The principles of right and wrong that are accepted by an individual or a social group. Sometime people may have a hierarchy of values; where some values are rated higher than others, which are considered to be of lesser importance. Our values may change over time or they could remain the same.

Bias: Preference for or likes, dislikes, interests, and/or priorities.

Cultural bias: Preferences, likes, and dislikes passed from one generation to another within one cultural group.

Intercultural bias: Preferences, likes, and dislikes that members of one group have for their own culture over the cultures of other groups.

Within-group bias: Preferences, likes, and dislikes of the members of a subculture for their own subgroup over other subcultures of their larger group.

Diversity: "The existence of variety in human expression, especially the multiplicity of mores and customs that are manifested in social and cultural life" (McAuliffe & Associates, 2008).

Ethnicity: "A characterization of a group of people who see themselves and are seen by others as having a common ancestry, shared history, shared traditions, and shared cultural traits such as language, beliefs, values, music, dress, and food" (Cokley, 2007).

Cultural differences are ETHNIC

- ❖ **E** Everyone has a culture

- ❖ **T** Take time to collect relevant cultural information

- ❖ **H** Hold all judgements.

- ❖ **N** Notice and negotiate differences in understanding

- ❖ **I** Involve cultural resources as appropriate

- ❖ **C** Collaborate to develop objectives and strategies.

Oppression: "Inequity is often a consequence of oppression, in that a group in power uses its advantages to keep other groups from accessing resources. Oppression is the condition of being subject to another group's power.

Prejudice: Typically, negative attitudes toward individuals or identified groups of individuals that are formed prior to the gathering of information or knowledge about the individuals or groups.

Racism: Acts of oppression based solely on race.

Worldview: Presuppositions and assumptions an individual hold about the makeup of his or her world; how a person perceives his or her relationship to the world (nature, institutions, other people, things, and so on) (Ibrahim, 1991). An individual's worldview is culturally learned.

BELIEFS SYSTEMS

There are three 'visions' within which people look to learn the 'truth' of things, including matters of fact and matters of value:

1. those centred in God's word (revelation);
2. those centred in the minds of men and women (reason); and
3. those decentred and dispersed within language, meaning and culture (relativism).

Belief systems serve in helping people understand their social world and can be a source of good. That is, they help people perceive, interpret, and predict events (e.g. predicting whether people will succeed or fail) and select courses of action (e.g. deciding whether to help a victim of misfortune)

Moreover, although people's belief systems may be stable over time, and have even been considered personality traits, some belief systems can change through personal experience.

DIFFERENT VIEWS

The first two concepts: stereotypes and generalisations all have the ability to have stereotypical views and to form generalisations about others. These stereotypical views and generalisations could be in relation to people who have experienced harmful practices or how have perpetrated such practices. It is important to therefore consider what some of these stereotypical views and generalisations are made by society that we might agree with. It is important that these views are challenged in a sensitive and caring way.

What is a Stereotype? Holding views regarding specific individuals and groups based on generally negative assumptions or accusations about their characteristics or behaviour. Stereotyped outlooks are mainly unsympathetic to those to whom they apply.

Our values, beliefs and attitudes will in some way influence those we work with. This is especially so in relation to those who engage in harmful health and cultural practices, you might be firmly opposed to them. Sometimes despite the best of intentions when working to help others we might engage in behaviour does further harm. One reason why this might occur is due to unconscious bias.

Unconscious bias refers to a bias that we are unaware of, and which happens outside of our control. It is a bias that happens automatically and is triggered by our brain making quick judgments and assessments of people and situations, influenced by our background, cultural environment and personal experiences.

One way to overcome unconscious biases is to challenge stereotypes. One stereotypical view amongst some is that harmful health and cultural practices only occur in Black and Minority Ethnic communities.

The Girl Generation work on developing a set of principles for organisations working to tackle Female Genital Mutilation offers a good guide for all to adhere to when working not only to tackle this issue but others as well. In your work it is important to adhere to the following principles:

- Avoid using underhand tactics or scaremongering
- Do not use imagery that will compromise the dignity or privacy of human subjects e.g. bloodied razors, pictures of private parts)
- Use language that will not compromise the dignity or privacy of human subjects and culture e.g. using words such as barbaric, uneducated, uncivilised)
- Use accurate information about health and cultural practices and ensure that the information you use comes from reliable sources
- Co-production is key: this means that getting survivors and communities involved as this means that you will not be talking at them.
- Have a wider understanding of the other issues affecting the groups you will be working with e.g. poverty, health and the impact this could have on the group
- Use a human rights approach: we all have a right to be protected from harm and abuse.

CULTURAL COMPETENCE

When working with others who are culturally different from oneself it is important to be aware of the steps you can take to learn more about their culture. The term used for this is called "cultural competence".

Cultural competence is being respectful of and responsive to the beliefs, practices and cultural and linguistic needs of diverse communities. There are five essential elements that contribute to an individual worker's, and a whole organisation's, ability to become more culturally competent. The professional or service must:

- Value diversity
- Have the capacity for cultural self-assessment
- Be conscious of the 'dynamics' inherent when cultures interact
- Institutionalise cultural knowledge, and
- Develop adaptations to service delivery reflecting an   understanding of diversity between and within cultures

Developing the skills and expertise through training can possibly inject a change in practice.

Whilst it is important for practitioners and organisations to be culturally competent there are limits to this move. Cultural competence will only contribute to an increase in knowledge and expertise about the culture of others. Cultural competence erroneously views cultural groups as homogenous and does not account for variations within groups. Furthermore, acquiring knowledge about the culture of others fails to recognise that practitioners do not approach a child with biased attitudes. It does not help practitioners to consider how their values, beliefs and attitudes influence how they have an effect on those they work with. It also fails to recognise that 'the ability to understand one's own culture is the stepping stone to being able to understand other cultures.

A better approach will be to become culturally competent and at the same time to be consciously aware of and reflect on how own morals, values, emotions and attitudes can affect the way we work with others. This involves what is called "cultural sensibility":

'The danger of making assumptions of this kind is clear. Cultural norms and models of behaviour can vary considerably between communities and even families.... The range of cultures and behavioural patterns it includes is so wide that it would be meaningless to make generalisations, and potentially damaging to an effective assessment of the needs of the child. The wisest course is to be humble when considering the extent of one's own knowledge about different 'cultures' and to take advice whenever it is available' (The Victoria Climbie Inquiry, Lord Laming 2003)

However, people of different cultural backgrounds often have to interact with each other. These interactions may lead to strong relationships that help build diverse communities capable of achieving substantial goals. For instance, it may be necessary to work effectively with people from divergent races or with those who speak a different language to promote economic development and health care within a community or secure a good education for children.

While it is important to learn about the cultures of other people to succeed in working together, one must first understand his own culture before he can appreciate any other. This understanding starts with recognition of the values, customs and world views passed down from grandparents or parents or those acquired from personal experiences while growing up in a given society. One can learn about culture by meeting people of other cultures, evaluating any biases towards other cultures, asking questions and reading

Cultural identity is important because it acts as a way to preserve history and provides individuals a place where they feel they belong. Cultural identity is established when a group of people continually follows the same sets of social norms and behaviour as those of earlier generations. An individual's cultural identity is influenced by factors such as ancestry, social class, educational level, family, language, political opinions and profession.

People with a strong sense of culture identity are more likely to feel a sense of security and belonging, according to the Social Report. People with a strong and defined cultural identity typically show positive outcomes in terms of education and health. They are more likely to have social networks to depend on for support, as well as to feel a sense of trust with people within those networks.

Many people identify culturally with a variety of subcultures, and cultural identity itself can change over time as the beliefs and behaviour of individuals and groups change. However, acknowledging the breadth of cultural identity is crucial to any efforts to move beyond racism and to bring about reconciliation between cultural groups.

Printed in the United States
By Bookmasters